QUEEN ELIZABETH II, THE GREAT

The Life of the Great Monarch OF England

C. J. Zaph

DISCLAIMER

TABLE OF CONTENTS

INTRODUCTION

We originated from dust, and we must go back to dust. The author of this book wanted to pay tribute to the late Queen Elizabeth II of the United Kingdom, who was a brilliant leader.

We need to value life as a gift with everything we have. Because tomorrow is not guaranteed, we only have today.

She was incredibly powerful, brave, and a naturally charismatic woman. Queens occasionally require a reminder of just how awesome they are.

We take it for granted because we believe that women should be doing it regardless of the sacrifices they make to protect our emotional and physical well-being.

It's time we gave every woman the respect they deserved and treated them like queens.

QUEEN ELIZABETH, THE GREAT

THE HISTORY OF THE MORNACHS

Alfred the Great, who initially controlled Wessex, one of the seven Anglo-Saxon kingdoms that later became modern England, is at the top of this list of current kings and queens of the Kingdom of England. While Alfred did not claim to control all of England, his reign marks the beginning of the first uninterrupted dynasty of rulers who did, the House of Wessex. Alfred began referring to himself as King of the Anglo-Saxons in the year 886.

Since the political union of the Kingdoms of England and Scotland on May 1st, 1707, there have been 13 British kings. Since March 24, 1603, England and Scotland have been personally united. The United Kingdom was established on January 1, 1801, following the union of the Kingdoms of Great Britain and Ireland.

- Anne Stuart is first on the list. She ruled the empire for seven years and 93 days, from 1 May 1707 to 1 August 1714. James II and VII and Anne Hyde welcomed her into the world at St. James's Palace on February 6, 1655. On July 28, 1683, she became engaged to George of Denmark, and they were wed at St. James's Palace. The couple had five kids together. She was on this planet for 49 years and 144 days.

Anne Stuart

- The next name on the list is George I, George Louis, from 1 August 1714 until 11 June 1727, a period of 12 years and 315 days; he was in charge of the empire. On May 28, 1660, in Leineschloss, he was born to Ernest Augustus of Brunswick-Lüneburg and Sofia of Hanover. He became engaged to Sophia Dorothea Brunskwick-Lüneburg-Celle on November 21st, 1682, and the two later married. Together, they had two children. He passed away on June 11, 1727, after a life span of 67 years and 14 days.

Art by Godfrey Kneller

- The third person on the list is George II, also known as George Augustus. He ruled the empire for 33 years and 126 days, from 11 June 1727 to 25 October 1760. George I and Sophia Dorothea of Brunswick-Lüneburg-Celle welcomed a child on October 30, 1683, at Herenhausen Palace. On August 22nd, 1705, he announced his engagement to Caroline of Brandenburg-Ansbach; the two eventually were hitched. Eight kids were born to them collectively. After 76 years and 350 days of existence, he died on October 25th, 1760.

By Thomas Hudson

- George III also called George William Fredric, follows. Between 22 September 1761 and 29 January 1820, he controlled the empire for 59 years and 97 days. Prince Fredrick and Augusta of Saxe-Gotha welcomed George III into the world on May 21, 1738, at Norfolk House. On September 8, 1761, he made known that he was going to marry Charlotte of Mecklenburg-Strelitz. 15 children were born in the union. On January 29, 1820, he passed away after 81 years and 239 days of life.

By Allan Ramsay

- The next is George IV, also known as George Augustus Fredric. He was in charge of the empire between 19 July 1821 and 26 June 1830, a period of 10 years and 149 days. On August 12, 1762, at St. James's Palace, George IV was welcomed into the world by George III and Charlotte of Mecklenburg-Strelitz. He announced his intention to wed Caroline of Brunswick-Wolfenbüttel on April 8, 1795. The union gave birth to one daughter. He died on June 26, 1830, having lived 67 years and 318 days.

Art by Thomas Lawrence

- The next is William IV, also known as William Henry. He was in charge of the empire between 8 September 1831 and20 June 1837, a period of 6 years and 360 days. On August 21, 1765, at Burkingham Palace, William IV was welcomed into the world by George III and Charlotte of Mecklenburg-Strelitz. He announced his intention to wed Adelaide of Saxe-Meiningen Kew Palace on 13 July 1818.The union gave birth to two daughters. He died on June 20, 1837, having lived 71 years and 303 days.

By Martin Archer Shee

- Victoria Alexandrina picked up the mantle and ruled 28 June 1838 and22 January 1901, aperiodof 63 years and 217 days. On 24 May 1819, at Kensington Palace, Victoria was welcomed into the world by Prince Edward, Duke of Kent and Strathern and Victoria of Saxe-Coburg-Saalfeld. She got married to Alex of Saxe-Coburg on 10 February1840 and had nine children. She died on January 22, 1901, having lived 81 years and 243 days.

By Franz Xaver

- The next is Edward VII, also known as Albert Edward. He was in charge of the empire between 9 August 1902 and 6 May 1910, a period of 9 years and 105 days. On November 9, 1841, at Buckingham Palace, he was welcomed into mortality by Victoria and Albert of Saxe-Coburg. He married Alexandra of Denmark at St. George's Chapel on 10 March 1863. The union gave birth to six children. He died on 6 May 1910, having lived 68 years and 178 days.

By Luke Fildes

- George VI, also known as George Ernest Fredrick Albert was in charge of the empire between 22 June 1911 and 20 January 1936, a period of 25 years and 260 days. On June 3, 1865, at Marlborough House, he was welcomed into mortality by Edward VII and Alexandra of Denmark. He grew and married Mary of Teck on 6 July 1893 and had six children. He died on 20th January 1936, having lived 70 years and 231 days.

By Luke Fildes

- George VI, also known as Albert Fredrick Arthur George was in charge of the empire between 12 May 1937 and6 February 1952, a period of 15 years and 58 days. On December 14, 1895, at Sandringham House, he was welcomed into mortality by Mary of Tek and George V. He married Elizabeth Bowes-Lyon on 26 April, 1923 and had two daughters. He died on 6 February, 1952, having lived 56 years and 54ays.

By Sir Gerald Kelly

- The title of the longest-serving monarch of all time was finally bestowed upon the Great Queen Elizabeth Alexandra Mary, who lived for 96 years, 140 days, and governed for 70 years, 215 days. She was the child of George VI and Elizabeth Bowes-Lyon. She had four kids after marrying Philip Mountbatten. She passed away on September 8, 2022, and will live on in our hearts always.

Sir Herbert James Gunn

THE QUEEN LOVED DOGS

Elizabeth has loved corgis her entire life; she has been enamored with them since she was a child. Elizabeth fell in love with Dookie, the Royal Family's first corgi, when she was a little princess. Dookie was adopted in 1933.

When she was 18 years old in 1944, her father gave her Susan, the first corgi she had owned herself. Susan would be the first corgi in the queen's extensive family tree of approximately 30 corgis.

The queen also produced dorgis by breeding corgis and dachshunds. This adorable cross-breed dog may have been the result of an unintentional encounter between Princess Margaret's dachshund and one of Elizabeth's corgis. Over the years, more than 10 dorgis were produced by the sisters' repeated mating of the dogs.

The queen reportedly planned to stop breeding corgis in 2015 because she didn't want to leave any behind when she passed away.

THE ROYAL LOVE STORY

The love between Queen Elizabeth and Prince Philip was timeless. Princess Elizabeth, the future queen, wed Lieutenant Philip Mountbatten on November 20, 1947.

On July 10, 1947, the adorable couple made their wedding plans public.

She was 21 years of age when she got engaged to her future husband of 26 years. After their magnificent royal wedding at Westminster Abbey on November 20, 1947, it's safe to conclude that the couple was destined for glory.

The Princess needed ration coupons to purchase the fabric for her wedding dress, demonstrating to the world that she would be a modest monarch.

A shared sense of humor is also a key component of their enduring connection; after all, Prince Philip is known for his sense of humor.

Instead of having a "professional qualification in something," the 99-year-old Duke of Edinburgh makes fun of the fact that he is the "fella who belongs to Mrs. Queen." The Duke commented another time of the incredible quality The Queen possessed. He said, "You can take it from me, the Queen has the quality of tolerance in abundance.

Their union could serve a lesson to anyone who wishes to have an enduring love life.

Queen Elizabeth and Prince Philip were the epitome of love and dedication when it came to enduring royal relationships.

Prince Philip was the Queen's constant companion and source of support during their courtship and marriage.

Sadly, their long-standing relationship came to an end on April 9, 2021, when the Palace announced that Prince Philip had passed away. The Queen, who was 96 years old, passed away sixteen months later. But even now, the story of their romance endures.

It is anticipated that The Queen and Prince Philip will be interred together in their ultimate resting place after she dies of old age.

Philip was laid to rest in the Royal Vault at St. George's Chapel, on the grounds of Windsor Castle, following his "no fuss" burial; however, this is merely his temporary resting place.

When the Queen passes away and is interred at the King George VI Memorial Chapel, his remains will be relocated to be placed next to hers.

The Queen's parents, King George VI and The Queen Mother, as well as her younger sister, Princess Margaret, will also be buried there, next to the pair.

Additionally interred there are Prince Albert and Queen Victoria.

Words can't express the love they had for themselves and their children. So, feel free to smile while translating the photos below.

Many idolize her union. She was a remarkable person.

THE QUEEN'S OFFSPRINGS

- Prince Charles

  Charles Philip Arthur George, the future Prince of Wales, was born on November 14, 1948. Charles was born in Buckingham Palace, even though his own children and three of his grandchildren were all born in the same hospital—the Lindo Wing at St. Mary's Hospital in London.

  Prince Charles' mother was crowned in 1953 when he was four years old. As a result of her royal duties, which included a six-month Commonwealth tour, she and Prince Philip traveled the world while Charles and his sister stayed at home with their caregivers. The queen "had been brought up in that method herself, after all, with her parents leaving her at home and delegating her entire schooling to a governess and home tutors," historian Robert

Lacy, who has worked as an advisor for The Crown, opened up.

Most royal biographers depict an isolated upbringing for the purportedly shy Charles, followed by years spent away from home at Gordonstoun boarding school in Scotland. At a polo match, Charles met Camilla Parker-Bowles, the woman he would ultimately marry and become an enthusiastic polo player. According to reports, Charles's decision to join the Royal Navy interrupted their marriage, and they later wed other individuals. Charles's marriage to Lady Diana Spencer was and continues to be a source of intense public interest.

Now 73, Prince Charles was previously the longest-serving heir apparent to the English throne in British history. He immediately ascended to the throne as King on September 8, 2022, when his mother passed away.

- Princess Anne, Prince Philip and Elizabeth's only daughter

Elizabeth and Philip stayed at Clarence House in London until 1953, where Anne Elizabeth Alice Louise was born on August 15, 1950. At the time of her birth, the 72-year-old princess, who is presently known as Anne, Princess Royal was Charles's rival for the throne. Later royal births have elevated Anne to the 14th position in the succession since that time.

Anne was a tot when her mother and father began leaving her and Charles at home for royal obligations, often for extended amounts of time. But she's publicly dismissed any narrative that paints Queen Elizabeth as emotionally distant.

She said: We may not have been overly demanding as children since we were aware of the time constraints and obligations placed on her as monarch in the tasks and journeys she had to do, but "In 2002, Anne talked to the BBC."But I don't think any of us ever had the slightest doubt that she loved us just like any other mother would have."

Princess Anne, like all British royals, is heavily influenced by the way the British media interprets her every gesture. Although descriptions of Anne's allegedly impolite behavior show a perhaps sexist discomfort with her frank demeanor, she was given the (quite harsh) epithet Her Royal Rudeness by some members of the press.

She spoke about her long-standing distaste for royal walkabouts in the 2018 BBC documentary The Queen: Her Commonwealth Story. "Sure, it becomes simpler, but tries to visualize. How many people appreciate entering a room filled with people they have never met before? "She spoke."Afterward, try a street. I doubt many young people would voluntarily offer to do it."

Princess Anne, like her brother Charles, has been married twice. She married Captain Mark Phillips in 1973, with which she shares children Peter Phillips and Zara Tindall. Anne and Philips separated in 1989. Shortly after their 1992 divorce, she remarried Vice Admiral Timothy Laurence, her current husband.

- Prince Andrew

  After giving birth to Princess Anne, Elizabeth went ten years without bearing any more children (being the Queen of England is a pretty time-consuming gig). Andrew Albert Christian Edward, better known as Prince Andrew, Duke of York, was born to Her Majesty at Buckingham Palace on February 19, 1960.

After prep school, he attended Gordonstoun, the same boarding school in Scotland that his father and older brother had attended. He was homeschooled until the age of eight.

In 1986, Prince Andrew wed Sarah "Fergie" Ferguson, with whom he had two daughters, Beatrice and Eugenie. In 1996, the couple decided to get divorced.

Sarah Fergie and Prince Andrew, 1986.

- Prince Edward, the queen’s youngest child Prince Edward Antony Richard Louis was the first of Elizabeth's children to be born in the delivery room with Prince Philip present, which was a significant shift from convention. She'd been keenly reading women's magazines that stressed the importance of involving fathers in childbirth and had become fascinated by the idea.

  More so than his brothers, Edward has stayed out of the public eye. His two children, James Viscount Severn and Lady Louise Windsor, were born to him and Sophie Rhys-Jones in 1999.

  At age 23, Edward was employed by Andrew Lloyd Webber's Useful Theatre Company as a production assistant. His entertainment-related endeavors sometimes weren't as successful. The Guardian referred to Edward's decision to enlist his family members in a one-time charity event modeled after the British game show it’s a Knockout as a "public-relations disaster."

Condolences

May the soul of the great Monarch rest in perfect peace with her ancestors.